THE HUSBAND SCHOOL
PRESENTS

The New Husband's Survival Guide

*The Secrets To A Happy Marriage
While Navigating Sex, Money And A Shared Bathroom*

BY **RICK RESNICK**   ILLUSTRATIONS BY **DAN FOOTE**

The Husband School™ Presents:
The New Husband's Survival Guide
The Secrets To A Happy Marriage While Navigating Sex, Money And A Shared Bathroom

Copyright © 2024 by Rick Resnick

The Husband School is a division of U.S. Explorers, LLC.

All rights reserved. No part of this book may be reproduced or used in any manner without written permission of the copyright owner except for the use of quotations in a book review. For more information, go to husbandschool.co.

This is a work of humor. The author is not a trained marriage counselor. You should consult with a professional when appropriate. Any perceived advice contained herein may not be suitable for your situation. Neither the author nor the publisher shall be liable for any personal or commercial damages.

Names, characters, places and incidents either are the product of the author's imagination or are used fictitiously. Any resemblance to actual persons, living or dead, events, or locales is entirely coincidental.

First paperback edition March 2025
First eBook edition March 2025

Illustrations by Dan Foote
Book design by Tom Carling, Carling Design, Inc.

ISBN 979-8-9912429-0-5 (paperback)
ISBN 979-8-9912429-1-2 (ebook)

www.husbandschool.co

TABLE OF CONTENTS

Introduction	**The Husband School**	4
Disclaimer	**It's Just A Joke**	7
Preface	**Buy This Book**	9
Chapter 0	**Getting to the Altar**	13
Chapter 1	**The Honeymoon Phase—Giddy Up!**	19
Chapter 2	**Rookie Mistakes—Staying Out Of The Penalty Box**	25
Chapter 3	**Girls Are Gross, Too—What "They" Won't Tell You**	33
Sidebar	**The Cycle of Wife**	38
Chapter 4	**Home Life—The Battle For Field Position**	41
Sidebar	**Cleanliness Compatibility Quiz**	48
Chapter 5	**The Bathroom—The Space-Time Continuum**	51
Sidebar	**"Where Is There Hair?" Quiz**	57
Chapter 6	**The Bedroom—Let The (Olympic) Games Begin**	59
Chapter 7	**Sex—The Keys To Repeat (Funny) Business**	65
Sidebar	**Your Wife's Monthly Visitor**	69
Chapter 8	**Social Life—It's Time To Start Seeing Other People**	73
Chapter 9	**Communication—Can You Speak Venusian?**	79
Sidebar	**Wife Translator**	84
Chapter 10	**Arguments—"My Wife Is Never Wrong"**	89
Sidebar	**Wife Hacks**	95
Chapter 11	**Money Matters—Ask The Magic 8 Ball**	99
Chapter 12	**Making Babies—The Parent Trap**	105
Conclusion	**Looking Back**	113

INTRODUCTION

The Husband School™

"Marriage is a wonderful institution ... but who wants to live in an institution?" —Groucho Marx, about 100 years ago

For centuries, the Big Wedding Industrial Complex has been indoctrinating girls and women, brainwashing them with images of beautiful brides and gorgeous grooms getting married in fairytale ceremonies, pledging love and devotion until death do they part.

We guys have been dragged along, often without realizing it.

You know the story. A dude is happily dating different women until one day he—somehow—finds himself in a monogamous relationship.

Before the unsuspecting guy knows it, the beguiling beauty has convinced him to get engaged. But when he proposes, the future groom is fully unprepared for the holy hell he has unleashed.

Who will save him? Spoiler: No one.

- His friends are just as clueless about marriage as he is.
- His older brother was never too bright to begin with.

▶ His father won't say a word. He's not looking for trouble.

In other words, it was every man for himself. Until The Husband School™ came along.

As recently as 2024, we could send people into space and solve Wordle in two. But we did NOT have an organization dedicated to educating the country's most vulnerable population: recently married (and soon-to-be married) young men.

That could NOT stand.

So, with the help of concerned citizens, we founded The Husband School. Our only goal is to help mankind. And make a lot of money.

What exactly is The Husband School? Well, think of us as a resource to humorously help husbands (and husbands-to-be) ride the rollercoaster of marriage. (*Visit us at husbandschool.co*)

The Husband School relies on a Husbands Panel, crowdsourcing and dubious research to provide guidance. We won't always have the answers, but based on our years of experience, we can provide a preview of what you might face in married life.

Even though you and your wife are a unique couple, it's pretty certain

THE NEW HUSBAND'S SURVIVAL GUIDE

that many husbands have already experienced what you're about to experience. And some have lived to tell the tale.

We have big plans for The Husband School. Online courses. Live events. Certifications. Hats and T-shirts. Board games. TV dinners. NFTs. But our first project is *The New Husband's Survival Guide*.

After all, you don't throw a T-shirt to a drowning man. You toss him a life preserver. Think of this book as a life preserver. If you read it, you might end up cold, wet and frightened … but you will still be alive!

Which means you'll still be able to buy our comfortable, cotton-blend T-shirts!

Some of the T-shirts feature our motto: UXOR MEA NON ERRAT. That's Latin for "My Wife Is Never Wrong." It's a message that has stood the test of time, from ancient Rome through today.

The sooner you learn it, the better off you'll be. Welcome aboard!

—*The Husband School Board of Trustees*

DISCLAIMER

It's Just A Joke

A Message From The Husband School:

This book is meant to be funny. It will occasionally succeed. Although our "humor" and "jokes" often rely on dated clichés and/or stereotypes about husbands, wives, in-laws, kids, circus clowns, etc., it is all meant in jolly good fun. Husbands are great! Wives are great! In-laws are, well, whatever.

Some men love ballet. And stay home with the kids. Some women love fantasy football. And run Fortune 500 companies. These days, many women even drive cars. We get it! Stop lecturing us. We're just trying to have a laugh or two, dammit.

Don't tell the kids this, but some couples live together and *(gasp)* aren't even married! If you are one of those live-in boyfriends, we consider you an "honorary husband." Huzzah!

And yes, we know that not all husbands marry women. Not all wives marry men. Love is love!

But we are focusing on what we know best, having once been clueless young men betrothed to bright young women who knew

THE NEW HUSBAND'S SURVIVAL GUIDE

what they wanted when they wanted it.

As inexperienced husbands, we were so naive. Even though it was all perfectly predictable, at the time we had NO IDEA what we were in for. Looking back, we would have benefited greatly from a trusted, go-to resource—a "survival guide" if you will.

Eureka! For a new generation of men, *The New Husband's Survival Guide* is that trusted resource.

Because if you can't trust an organization called The Husband School, who can you trust?

So, enjoy the book! Enjoy the journey! You'll thank us later. Trust us.*

---

* But use your head, man. We're not trained marriage counselors. We're not trained at ANYTHING. We don't guarantee that any of our clever little tips will work with your wife. They could backfire terribly. You know her a lot better than we do. You're the one who married her!

PREFACE

Buy This Book

If you are reading this, you are probably recently married. Or about to get married. Or, perhaps, about to move in with your girlfriend.

First of all, congratulations! She is amazing! Smart. Funny. And smokin' hot. Well done!

Second, a few quick questions: Are you sure marriage was the right move? No, really. What were you thinking? How well do you truly know this woman??

DO YOU HAVE ANY IDEA WHAT YOU ARE IN FOR???

Let's answer the last question first: No, you do not.

You have NO IDEA what you are in for.

Luckily, *The New Husband's Survival Guide* is in your hands! And if you BUY THIS BOOK—instead of just skimming it in a bookstore, or borrowing it from one of your smarter friends—not only might you survive marriage, you could even emerge somewhat unscathed.

THE NEW HUSBAND'S SURVIVAL GUIDE

(Past performance is no guarantee of future success. Results may vary.)

We at The Husband School have spared almost no expense to help you navigate the obstacle course of married life.

Some editorial highlights include:

- **Rookie Mistakes**—Avoid them to stay out of the penalty box
- **The Cycle of Wife**—How things change over time
- **Winning Bedroom Battles**—This isn't about sex … it's the struggle to secure sleeping chamber serenity
- **Wife Translator**—What she says isn't always what she means
- **Losing Arguments Gracefully**—You are going to lose, so do it right
- **Wife Hacks**—Amazing tricks that will delight your wife and make you a hero (for a little while, at least)

For roughly the price of a Big Mac, large fries, two Red Bulls and a pack of Twinkies (a.k.a. "lunch"), all of this vital knowledge can be yours. And you can't put a price on happiness.

As you prepare to sit down and read our guide—whether on the couch, in bed, or on the toilet—let us start with a little secret to get you in the right frame of mind: *You have to laugh.*

Buy This Book

You have to laugh when you find out that your wife (or live-in girlfriend) is not exactly who you thought she was. When you realize that she is just as flawed as you are. And equally as annoying.

She won't be able to keep up the "perfection" act forever. We know from experience.

(Author's note: This book is NOT autobiographical. My wife IS perfect. The included observations aren't mine. They are the result of detailed insight from our Husbands Panel, rigorous internet browsing and traditional American folklore. Then we sprinkled in a few apocryphal stories for extra flavor.)

If you can laugh at the unexpected discoveries of cohabitation … if you can appreciate the differences that you and your wife bring to this union … and, most importantly, if you BUY THIS BOOK, you *will* figure out this marriage thing. Almost certainly.

Either way, no returns! The Husband School's alternate motto is CAVEAT EMPTOR. We're keeping the $17.95 *(softcover MSRP)*.

—Rick Resnick, Headmaster, The Husband School

CHAPTER 0

Getting To The Altar

Even though this is *The New Husband's Survival Guide*, no law in America prohibits non-husbands from reading it.

Plenty of impressionable young men—many of whom are merely *contemplating* marriage—will be scouring this book as they attempt to do a cost-benefit analysis regarding their current significant other.

So, for those of you not yet married, we offer this BONUS "prequel" chapter to use if/when you decide you want to "pop the question."

That question, of course, is "What the hell should I do?"

We're here to help! Here are "8 Easy Steps for Getting to the Altar," if you are so inclined:

Step 1—Understand Each Other's Values
How well do you really know this woman? Sure, you've seen her unusual tattoo, hidden away in a *very* private place. But that's not enough.

You'll need to have "the talk" about what life might look like. Will you live in the city or the suburbs? Have kids or not? Dogs or cats?

Is she willing to support you financially while you work on your novel? Will boys' golf weekends still be allowed? Does she want to have sex merely SEVEN times per week or significantly more often?

If you aren't aligned on these key questions, marriage experts consider that a "yellow flag," which means "you're screwed." But if you like what you hear, keep going ...

Step 2—Meet Each Other's Most Important People

Make a point to go out in a group with her closest friends. Meet and mingle with her relatives at family events. Get introduced to her co-workers, hairdresser, pilates instructor, life coach and psychiatrist.

If the majority of these people are not complete assholes, and her mother is objectively good-looking, then you are on the right path.

And if your friends think your girlfriend is pretty cool, you are ready for the next big step.

Step 3—Go On A Trial Honeymoon

Spend a week away together, just the two of you. Pick a location with great restaurants, interesting museums and vibrant nightlife. Go shopping together. Hit the hotel's hot tub. Order room service. Get plenty of quarters for the vibrating bed. Have fun!

And if you still like each other after the hassle of traveling, being

Getting To The Altar

stuck together 24/7 for a full week AND sharing a bathroom, congratulations! Proceed to Step 4.

Step 4—Ask For Her Parents' Permission To Get Married

Really? Are we still doing this in the 21st century? Isn't getting married a decision solely between you and her?

Technically, yes. But be practical. Do you want her parents to like you? Pay for the wedding? Let you two stay at their Florida condo and ride those awesome Jet Skis®? Of course!!

So swallow your pride, humble yourself and do what you have to do. It will be excellent practice for the marriage.

Step 5—Buy The Engagement Ring

Size doesn't matter? That's a lie with engagement rings, too. You've got one shot to get this right, buddy. Don't try to take the cheap way out.

Years ago, the helpful folks in the diamond industry kindly offered guidance on how much a prospective groom should spend on the ring: three months' salary. In other words, 25% of your annual pay.

For someone making $80,000, that would be TWENTY THOUSAND DOLLARS for a friggin' ring!

But think of it this way. If you amortize the ring over 50 years, that's only $1.09 a day. Do you love the woman that much or not, Romeo?

Step 6—Arrange The Proposal
It wasn't that long ago that you would give your girlfriend's father a couple of chickens, and you'd be engaged. In modern times, however, it's a lot more complicated.

In reality, the proposal has become as important as the wedding. It's her chance to get likes on Instagram while proving to her doubting friends that you really aren't a loser.

Luckily, the proposal is pretty straightforward. Just make sure you keep everything a secret while coordinating with all her family members and closest friends to create the picture-perfect social media-worthy moment. And while it must be a complete surprise, don't make it too much of a surprise, because the bride-to-be has to look sensational.

Here's a handy checklist of things that must be included in the photographs: (You DID book a photographer, right? ... Right?)
- The bride-to-be (in full makeup, perfect hair and nails)
- You (on bended knee, with a glistening ring)
- A lake
- Swans
- A gazebo
- A violin player

Getting To The Altar

- A marching band
- All of her family and friends, hidden, beaming with delight

Oh, and make sure it doesn't rain. That would ruin her hair.

Step 7—Organize The Bachelor Party

Go to Vegas. Or some local strip club. Have fun with your buddies. Whatever. Your best man can figure that out.

Feel free to include your dad. But DEFINITELY do not invite your future father-in-law. He does NOT want to know what kind of deviant you are.

Step 8—Plan The Wedding

Remember how we said the proposal has become as important as the wedding? We lied. The wedding is "the most important night of her life." Don't. Eff. It. Up.

Just say yes to everything she wants* and you will have a chance of surviving.

On the wedding day, you are simply a prop. Don't forget your role!

Once again, it will be excellent practice for the marriage.

---

*According to federal law, the groom is allowed to request up to three minor provisions, such as "Please spell my name correctly on the invitation," "No carrot cake wedding cake!" or "Do NOT play 'The Chicken Dance.'" Other than that, keep quiet.

CHAPTER 1

The Honeymoon Phase Giddy Up!

The wedding is over. What a night!

Sure, Uncle Stanley drank too much and caused a scene. And that asparagus dish was iffy. But other than that, it was perfect. Your wife looked like an angel. You were surrounded by your closest friends and family. And the gift haul was massive.

Huzzah!

So … what happens now?

It's time for the "Honeymoon Phase." No, that is NOT the same as the "honeymoon." Let us explain.

For many couples, the wedding will be followed by a "honeymoon," a getaway vacation, often to someplace warm with umbrella drinks. Those all-inclusive resorts are pretty sweet.

That's different than the "Honeymoon Phase," which is the state of near-constant giddiness you'll feel now that the two of you are husband and wife. According to brides.com, the Honeymoon Phase can last anywhere from six months to two years.

I'd definitely bet the under.

During the Honeymoon Phase, you'll imagine little pink hearts floating in the air every time you glance at your new bride. You'll call each other pet names, like "Snookums" and "Honey Biscuit." You won't be able to keep your hands off each other, and that new bed will get quite a workout.

To you, she's perfect! To her, you're perfect! (Narrator: You will both find out otherwise.)

Everything is fantastic. That spaghetti sauce on her chin is so cute! Her snoring at night is adorable! Going clothes shopping together is such a blast!

This is a time when life is full of unlimited possibilities. So, enjoy it! Explore your relationship. Have fun. Have LOTS of sex!

Live, laugh, love!

But do NOT set expectations too high—or you will be living up to them for 50 years. Set some boundaries! Here are some crucial watch-outs:

The Honeymoon Phase

Chores: Be a man and do your share. Now and then, pick up the vacuum. Load the dishwasher. Go get some groceries. But do NOT sneak out of bed in the middle of the night to dust and straighten up the place so she wakes up to a neat-and-tidy home.

Once you show her you can do it, it will become part of your permanent job description.

Presents: Yes, you MUST get gifts for all of the "big" days (i.e. her

THE NEW HUSBAND'S SURVIVAL GUIDE

birthday, Valentine's Day, wedding anniversary, engagement anniversary, first-date anniversary, meeting anniversary, etc.). And you will get HUGE bonus points for occasionally bringing home flowers for no particular reason. But don't overdo it.

One hapless hubby started buying roses for his wife EVERY Friday—and he was stuck forever. Talk about diminishing returns, the flowers became more expected than appreciated. There was less and less, er, bang for the buck. If you know what I mean.

Kind gestures: A successful marriage depends on giving more than you take. So get up and get the aspirin when your wife has a headache. Go scrape the ice off her car windshield. Make reservations at the Thai place across town.

But do NOT open the car door for her. Or make a habit of serving breakfast in bed. Or regularly offering foot massages.* You're not an indentured servant, for crying out loud.

Time together: Sure, you want to spend EVERY waking moment with your newlywed

The Honeymoon Phase

wife. Do NOT. Make sure to carve out time alone with your guy friends.

Two reasons: 1.) You and your bros will otherwise grow apart, and you will certainly need them once the Honeymoon Phase ends, and 2.) The more time you spend alone with "Snookums," the more time she has to notice that you really aren't so marvelous.

At some point, you'll realize that the Honeymoon Phase has ended. (Check your spreadsheets. Has sexual activity dropped by about 80%? Yep, the giddiness bubble has popped.) But don't worry.

When the Honeymoon Phase is over, the long-term relationship finally begins. And that's great! Almost certainly.

---

*Regular foot massages are allowed if, and only if, your wife is pregnant.

CHAPTER 2

Rookie Mistakes
Staying Out Of The Penalty Box

While you are floating through the just-described Honeymoon Phase, your heart will be aflutter. But your brain will be on the blink.

And dreaded Rookie Mistakes will be lurking around every corner.

These errors in judgment can make even the most well-intentioned husband look like a total schmuck. Not only will you end up in the marital penalty box for days, but these blunders might be remembered—and recounted—for decades.

The Husband School is dedicated to eradicating Rookie Mistakes. Let's prepare you for some husband traps you may face. Such as …

1. "Does This Make Me Look Fat?"
You may think this happens only in sitcoms. But it is very real.

Your wife will try on a new dress, blouse, sweater, jacket, bracelet, etc., and express concern that the object creates a mysterious and incorrect perception of weight gain.

"Does this make me look fat?" (Or its cousin, "Do I look fat in this?")

If you answer this question, you are toast. Do NOT answer. As a new husband, there is only one proper reaction to being asked this question:

Fake your own death.

Then, in a couple of weeks, after you reappear in remarkably good health, she will be so happy to see you that she will have forgotten the question entirely. Problem solved!

2. Listening To Her Problem—And Trying To Solve It

Your wife is on the couch, steaming mad. She's angry at a friend, who has just ruined her plans. As a caring new husband, you ask what's wrong. You listen intently and nod your head.

You are doing great.

As the scenario is being described, you devise a perfect solution to save the day. Then you generously share your quick fix.

You are an idiot. Now she is angrier at you than at that friend.

Why? Because wives do NOT want you to solve the problem. They just want you to listen, shake your head and agree with them.

Rookie Mistakes

Just nod often and keep your mouth shut. Then sneak away as quickly as possible.

3. "Calm Down"
Your wife is upset. She sounds frantic. She doesn't know what to do. You want to help her get back on an even keel, so she can get her thoughts together and solve the issue.

So you say it. The dreaded "C-word."

"Honey, CALM down. It will be okay."

Oh, you poor fool. Once again, you have made yourself the villain.

Despite all of our proprietary research, The Husband School can't fully explain the "Calm Down" Effect on women. When a guy says it to another guy, it's perfectly fine.

After you say it to your wife, head directly to the box. It's a major penalty.

4. "You're Just Like Your Mother"
Dude. You didn't just say that, did you?

THE NEW HUSBAND'S SURVIVAL GUIDE

Damn, you need a lot more help than we originally thought.

5. The Appliance Trap

Your wife says she really, truly wants that amazing new vacuum cleaner for her birthday. And she means it. So you go to get it.

Until you realize it's a trap.

Because whether it's two years from now or 20, the story will emerge that *you bought your wife a vacuum cleaner for her birthday*. And the part about her really, truly wanting it will be COMPLETELY forgotten.

You will look like an ass. Even your future grandkids will be embarrassed for you.

Get her a sweater instead. It's so much safer.

6. "Do You Like This Outfit?"

Stay focused. Keep it simple. The answer is "YES!"

If you must be more expansive, "YES, dear!" is acceptable. Do not stray further.

7. "Do Whatever You Want"

When your wife says, "Do Whatever You Want," she does NOT mean "Do Whatever You Want."

If you are smart, you will do the OPPOSITE of whatever you want.

And that will be the right move.

8. "Do You Think [My Friend] Is Attractive?"

Your wife has some hot friends. Try not to look at them. And definitely do NOT talk about them.

At some point, your wife will ask you, "Do you think [random friend] is pretty?"

This is a trap.

If you say, "No, not really," you have just insulted her friend. Not great.

If you say, "Yeah, I guess she is okay," your wife will envision you sleeping with her now *ex-friend*. And she won't trust you to leave the house. Really not great.

So what do you do? See Rookie Mistake No. 1. The same solution applies. Good luck!

Honorable Mention

Here are some other Rookie Mistakes that the Husbands Panel shared from their own experiences:

- Not listening intently to a story you've heard several times before. Which usually happens when the game is on.

- Overlooking her "I'm fine" or "I'm okay" response. It's not fine. It's not okay. Address it and buckle up.

- Assuming that you will be having sex all the time. You won't be.

- Thinking you will be able to play golf. Nope. Golf is out. You're not going to be gone for six hours on a Saturday or Sunday. Not happening.

- Giving an honest answer to, "Do you like this color (of paint, carpet, pillow, etc.)?" The right answer is always, "I like it if you like it."

- Complaining about how long her stories take, even if she repeats herself and throws in thousands of extraneous facts.

- Forgetting how sensitive she is to any slightly negative feedback. You could say 500 positives and she will hear only the one barely critical thing.

- Failing to effusively compliment an outfit. By doing that, you are effectively criticizing said outfit.

- Bringing up politics with your wife's Uncle Marvin.

Rookie Mistakes

- Taking "Sit back and relax. I got it" literally. She really doesn't want you to sit back and relax.

- Not fully understanding the risk of liking an ex-girlfriend's Instagram post.

- Correcting her when she is factually wrong. You may win the battle. You will lose the war.

- Complaining about dinner when she cooks. Do you want her to stop cooking? Forever?

- Going to sleep immediately following an argument, without coming to a resolution. The next day will be much worse, we promise.

CHAPTER 3

Girls Are Gross, Too
What "They" Won't Tell You

As a man, you KNOW that guys are gross. You've been around them forever, whether with brothers, school friends, college roommates, Army buddies, etc. And these guys are, quite simply, revolting.

They are dirty and smelly and rude and crude—and you're okay with that. Guys are meant to be disgusting.

But girls, we were taught at a young age, are sugar and spice and everything nice. Girls are clean and smell good. And they stay that way for life.

How would we know any better? Growing up, your mother was always a proper lady. (Around you, anyway.) If you had sisters, they were most certainly annoying, but at least they smelled okay.

Well, my friend. It's time to tell you the truth. It's time to reveal the thing that catches most new husbands completely unprepared.

Girls are gross, too.

In fact, depending on the wife, she might be more disgusting than many of your frat brothers.

Don't shoot the messenger, man. We're just trying to help!

You will see things you have never imagined. In the hamper. In the toilet. In the car. And yes, your beautiful blushing bride will have created each of those crimes against humanity.

The list of grossness is long. Many of the infractions are similar to what your buddies do. Some are much worse.

Listen, when your wife pulls at an underwear wedgie, she can do it from BOTH the front and the back. Guys can't do that.

At the risk of freaking you out, let's check our non-exclusive list. (*Non-exclusive* means there are even more things that aren't on our list.)

Sounds: Unlike you, your wife can burp, fart AND queef. (Warning: Doing all three simultaneously can lead to implosion.) Even if she is smaller than you, your wife can out-decibel you. It's remarkable actually. And did we mention snoring?

At the beginning, your wife will limit most of these sounds around you. But by your first anniversary, any decorum is out the window. At that point, she also might be cursing like a trucker on a regular basis.

Girls Are Gross, Too

Smells: Oh, lord. The smells. You find out quickly that the smell of passed gas is not a function of gender, it's more about the food consumed. So, if your wife drinks protein shakes or likes to do a "cleanse," you might face a hazmat situation before you know it.

And when she starts farting in bed, under the covers, the smell amplification levels multiply exponentially.

That's just the start of it. Remember your camp buddies with the stinky feet, the horrible morning breath and the occasionally shocking body odor? Well, your wife has all three. Enjoy!

Oh, and girls poop, too. Fun fact: Girl doody doesn't smell any better than boy doody.

Sights: This is where it really gets bad.

There is a very good chance that one day you will casually waltz into the bathroom, lift the lid … and recoil in horror. "IS THAT AN ANIMAL SACRIFICE IN THE TOILET?!?!"

No, silly. It's just a bloody women's hygiene

product that she forgot to flush. Sure, you'll be scarred for life, but what doesn't kill you makes you stronger.

Sometimes, instead of the Red Wedding, you'll lift the lid and be surprised by a round of brown. As in a toilet bowl full of skid marks. Poop punctuation marks. Shit shrapnel.

Apparently, one flush wasn't enough for your darling's doo-doo. Yay!

Back on dry land, one day you'll be doing the laundry and discover your wife's red-stained underwear, caked with dried blood. Once you catch your breath, you'll think, "Wow. We should have bought that new and improved Tide."

Slightly less gross, but more pervasive, your wife's hair will be EVERYWHERE. We'll get to that later.

Finally, after she gets to know you well enough, she will use her car the way she feels most comfortable. As a garbage can.

A half-eaten sandwich. Candy bar wrappers. Make-up containers. Assorted clothing. Ketchup packets. Dirty tissues. Dry cleaning bags. Juice containers. Plastic utensils. Banana peels. Empty Coke Zero cans. Toenail clippings.

Yep. She's a keeper!

Girls Are Gross, Too

Secrets: Women do things in secret they won't dare tell you. They don't necessarily tell their friends. But for some reason, they will tell Reddit. Here are a few:

- Pick their nose
- Pee in the shower
- Smell their own farts—and admire them
- Wear dirty clothes out of the hamper
- Wear the same bra for weeks
- Enjoy popping their zits
- Pick their nails
- Bite their nails
- Do mustache control
- Hunt for ear wax
- Pick dead skin off their feet
- Smell-check their armpits
- Use perfume to mask the smell of dirty clothes
- Clog the toilet with jumbo poops

The list goes on and on. (Some are too gross for us to even type.) And after the *Fifty Shades of Grey* phenomenon, your wife is also likely to be interested in pornography.

So, at the very least, you two have that in common!

SIDEBAR

The Cycle of Wife

This handy chart explains how life with the missus can change over time.

	Relationship Phases			
	Dating	Engaged	Honeymoon Phase	Settled In
Date Night	Trendy nightclubs	Friends' parties	Fancy restaurants	"What time does Cracker Barrel open?"
Her Bedroom Attire	Nothing	Fleur du Mal lingerie	Cozy Earth pajamas	Dick's Sporting Goods sweats
Sex	Hot and heavy	Passionate	Romantic	"Can we schedule something for next Saturday?"
Her Body Hair	Practically none	Still barely any	Legs are only half shaved	Legs are completely unshaven, porcupine-like armpits … and is that a hint of a mustache?
Her Body Noises	Cute hiccups	Quiet little burps	Occasional belches	Farts that are louder than Uncle Phil's after a chili cook-off
Her Pooping	Won't even acknowledge having a digestive system	Does it on the sly	Demands privacy	She wakes you up specifically to show off her massive deuce

The Cycle of Wife: Date Night

CHAPTER 4

Home Life
The Battle For Field Position

With marriage comes the opportunity to create a home together. So romantic, right?

First, you make the home. Then, you share the home. But neither is straightforward, because you two won't ever fully agree on either part.

Do both spouses have an equal say in the matter? What do you think?

Hundreds of decisions—some large, most quite small—determine what your home will look like and how it will function. Each decision indicates who is gaining the upper hand.

You yield in one area and (try to) stand firm in another. Push and pull. Pull and push. You may never win, but you'll never stop battling for field position.

In a war of attrition, the key is to pick your battles wisely. For example: If you agree with keeping all of those unnecessary throw pillows on the couch, she might let you control the TV remote. For a while.

THE NEW HUSBAND'S SURVIVAL GUIDE

Make The Home

To make a house a home, decoration is needed. That includes furniture. And stuff on the walls. To be clear: Your old stuff will NOT cut it.

That futon you've had since college? Gone.

Your sports posters and that amazing signed football helmet? Into the basement. Or a closet. Or long-term storage.

Why? Your wife has the answer: "It isn't our aesthetic."

Oh, we have an aesthetic? Well, YOU don't, but your wife does. And now it's yours, too!

But that's okay. She has style. You do not.

When you are asked, "Do you like the color of this paint (or carpet, pillow, etc.)?", the safest answer is, "I like it if you like it."

When you are asked, "Do you like this piece of furniture (or painting, carpet, knickknack, etc.)?", the best answer is, "If it's our aesthetic."

See, you're learning!

You WILL be involved with the furniture—if assembly is required.

For example: You get to put the IKEA furniture together. If you can do that while dropping fewer than five f-bombs, you are a legend. But I'd bet the over.

Share The Home

Good news. This is where you can win an occasional battle! Choose wisely, because there is a LONG list of battles to be contested. Here are a few:

The Thermostat
You want the Arctic, she wants the tropics. Giving her a gift certificate for a bunch of new sweaters might give you an edge.

The TV Remote
You want to watch the game, she wants to watch ANOTHER Hallmark movie. The short-term fix: Stream the game on your phone.

The long-term genius solution: Coax her into becoming a fan of your teams. Then she'll want to watch the game, too.

THE NEW HUSBAND'S SURVIVAL GUIDE

The Streaming Soundtrack

You love her, but not her taste in music? Well, get ready to spar over Spotify, plead about Pandora and argue about Apple Music. That's because you'll be bickering about whose playlists get priority. See, she doesn't like your music much either.

SPECIAL BONUS: This is an issue in both the home AND the car.

Tradition says that on the road, the driver controls the tunes. But if you do most of the driving, don't expect old customs to save you. And when it comes to home streaming, she can argue that the music is part of the aesthetic. Which, of course, is hers.

The Division Of Chores

Even today, some things are still considered "man's work"—like removing spiders, taking out the garbage and fixing the toilet handle. But everything else is up for grabs.

If your wife is a good cook, and she enjoys doing it, cooking is "hers." Then you can be in charge of the dishwasher. Which is great, because you have a specific system to maximize dishwasher efficiency and she HAS NO IDEA where anything goes.

PRO TIP: Regarding other chores—like cleaning, vacuuming and doing the laundry—harness the power of being really, really bad at something. If you botch these tasks a few times, your aggravated wife

Home Life

may eventually decide it's easier for her to just do them herself.

That's a win! But be careful: If you complain even once about how she does a chore that you're avoiding, that hot potato is certainly coming back your way.

The Clutter Factor

You know how folks declutter their homes before having company to make it seem like they aren't complete slobs? Well, that's what your wife was doing with you before you were living together.

And now her true colors are shining through.

She has stuff EVERYWHERE. Her stuff has stuff. It has a stranglehold on the place.

Solutions? Start with a gentle, honest conversation about how the clutter leaves you unsettled. It's not her, it's you.

If that doesn't work, suggest a few clutter-free zones to serve as a foothold of sanity.

If that doesn't work, throw some money at the problem. Hire a professional declutterer and have them teach you both a system for how to stay tidy.

If that doesn't work, throw more money at the problem. Buy a second home, just for her stuff. (Or yours!)

The Pet Protocol

You newlyweds are ready for the pitter-patter of little feet! Just not human feet. It's time to get a pet. Are you dog people or cat people?

Let's say you get a dog. Congrats! You will love your new fur baby.

But is the dog allowed on the couch? (You will have dog hair on your clothes forever.) Is the dog allowed in the bed? (Your sleep and sex life will both be painfully obstructed.) And whose turn is it to take Fido out in the rain?

When did life get so complicated?

The Man Cave
Now that you're married, you're ready for a cool "man cave" where you can be a "guy" doing "guy things." Good luck with that. When you are just starting out, the odds are that your home won't have a dedicated bro zone.

You're going to have to get creative. The garage? The basement? Maybe that broom closet has enough room for a folding chair?

One way or the other, you WILL need to carve out some space for yourself. Because, as we're about to find out, you will NOT be finding that space in the bathroom or the bedroom.

SIDEBAR

Cleanliness Compatibility Quiz

The questions below will help you determine if you and your spouse are on the same page regarding levels of cleanliness and propriety. Both of you should take the test individually and write down your answers without sharing.

After that, compare notes to predict your fate.

You and the missus earn points when you both pick the same answer to a question. Each question is worth 10 points (unless otherwise indicated).

Scale:
- 81-100 points   Rejoice: Harmonious living awaits
- 61-80 points   Warning: Some friction ahead
- 41-60 points   Danger: Cleanliness mismatch!
- 0-40 points   RED ALERT: Have you considered separate homes?

1. **How long can dirty dishes stay in the sink?**
   - Two hours
   - Two days
   - No limit, we'll just get takeout

2. **How often should bed sheets be washed and changed?**
   - Once a week
   - Once a month
   - Depends on how "busy" we get in that bed, if you catch my drift

3. **Are food splatters in the microwave a problem?**
   - No, they remind me of modern art
   - No, the radiation kills all germs
   - Yes, grab a Clorox wipe, you slob!

4. **Are any of these acceptable in bed? (2 points each)**
   - Clipping toenails   (Y or N)
   - Digging out ear wax with a Q-tip (Y or N)
   - Flossing your teeth   (Y or N)
   - Eating a full tube of Pringles (Y or N)
   - Grading the smell of your farts (Y or N)

5. **How often should the toilet be scrubbed?**
   - Once a day
   - Once a week
   - Just flush it a few extra times, and it'll be fine

6. **How many times can you wear a pair of jeans before they need washing?**
   - One time
   - Three times
   - Jeans can be washed?

7. **Is it okay for dresser drawers to be left open?**
   - No, it's not good for my OCD
   - No, you can get hurt bumping into the corners
   - No, did you grow up in a barn?

8. **How often is dusting necessary?**
   - Once a week
   - Once a month
   - What is "dusting"?

9. **If you drop an Oreo on the kitchen floor, can you still eat it?**
   - No, that's gross
   - Maybe, it depends on how dirty the floor is (see "five-second rule")
   - Yes, I am NOT wasting an Oreo

10. **Are "hair monsters" stuck to the shower walls a problem?**
    - No, it's just hair
    - Yes, it's like showering with Sasquatch
    - OMG, I'm gonna have a heart attack next time

Losing The Space Race

CHAPTER 5

The Bathroom
The Space-Time Continuum

They say that marriage is a 50-50 proposition. But that doesn't apply to the bathroom.

When it comes to space and time in the lav, equality goes, well, right down the toilet.

Based on The Husband School's proprietary research—using focus groups, regression analysis, carbon dating and the Pythagorean theorem—wives get, on average, about 80% of bathroom storage space. That leaves husbands with around 20%.

Is this fair? Well, let's crunch the numbers.

Here's what you, the husband, have to store in the restroom:

Toothbrush, deodorant, shaving cream, a razor and (if you were raised properly) dental floss. In the shower, it's soap and shampoo.

Seven items.

THE NEW HUSBAND'S SURVIVAL GUIDE

Here's what your wife has to store in the bathroom:

Toothbrush, toothpaste (shared), deodorant, shaving cream, a razor, dental floss, soap and shampoo (x5). And …

Face wash, face scrub, face toner, face mist, face masks, face brush, facial rollers, facial pore primer, nasal strips, concealer, beauty blender, sunscreen serum, hyaluronic acid serum …

Anti-aging repair serum, moisturizer, daily water cream, overnight sleeping cream, foundation, blush, gradual tanning lotion, bronzer, pimple patches, acne cream, highlighting pen …

Eyeshadow, eyeliner stencil, eyebrow stamp, eyelash curler, eyelash conditioner, eyebrow volumizer, eyebrow gel, mascara, eye masks, eye drops, false eyelashes, eyelash applicator …

Body lotion, body oil, body butter, body exfoliants, perfume, healing ointment, antibiotic ointment, hand cream, baby powder, astringent …

Makeup powder, makeup brushes, brush cleaning mat, makeup sponge, makeup removing wipes, makeup removing balm, makeup setting spray, makeup bag, makeup mirror, cotton balls, cotton swabs, tweezers, lipsticks (x10), lip liners, lip gloss, lip plumper, lip balm, lipstick mask …

The Bathroom

Hair mask, hair serum, hair conditioner, hair rinse, dry shampoo, dry styler, hair spray, hair gel, hair mousse, hair perfector, curl activator, curl revitalizer, hair color kit, anti-humidity spray, bonding oil …

Hair dryer, curling iron, flat iron, hairbrush, detangling comb, detangling spray, scalp massager, sleep cap, hair scrunchies, hair clips, bobby pins …

Teeth whiteners, floss threaders, water flosser, mouthwash, tongue scraper, breath strips …

Nail polish (x10), nail separators, nail polish holder, nail polish remover, nail strengthener, nail file, nail clippers, cuticle stick, cuticle remover, cuticle oil, press-on nails …

Foot powder, foot cream, heel guards, pumice stone, tampons, menstrual pads, panty liners, bath cloth, body wash, shower cap, depilatory, styptic pencil …

Aspirin, ibuprofen, acetaminophen, Midol, cold medicine, antihistamine, antacids, antiseptic spray, aloe gel, bandages and a thermometer.

That's 161 items, or thereabouts. Each one is vitally important.

Beauty is pain, boys. It's not easy to look that good.

Based on the math, your wife has 96% of the stuff and 80% of the space. So it clearly is unfair. *To her.*

Also, with 96% of bathroom items, your wife will need the large majority of bathroom *time*. The length and complexity of her beauty routines are beyond male comprehension.

If you both need to leave for work each morning, bathroom scheduling will be essential. Miss your time slot and you could end up taking a sponge bath in the kitchen sink.

In addition to the bathroom space-time continuum, there are several other potty pain points to prep for:

Hair, Hair, Everywhere
One Husbands Panel member says he extracts a ferret-sized hair mass out of the shower drain each month. And that's just the beginning of where your wife's hair will be. *(See the "Where is There Hair?" quiz after this chapter.)*

Potty Privacy Pact
Early in your marriage, one or both of you will likely have Shy Bowel Syndrome and insist on being given a wide berth in the bathroom. You're better off that way. You have *plenty* of years down the road to disgust each other.

The Bathroom

Aroma Ambush

The downside to you and your wife's stealth pooping missions is that the other spouse might not know when they are entering a hazmat situation. Living together comes with the responsibility to deal with your own stink.

For humanity's sake, open a window. Turn on the fan. Light a match. But do something. If it's just the two of you, it's easy to ID the culprit.

Toilet Seat Etiquette

Did you know that women pee while sitting down? It's true! As a result, they want the toilet seat down every time they use the potty. Which means husbands are required to put the toilet seat down after they are done whizzing.

You might say to yourself, "My wife has hands. Can't she just put the toilet seat down when she goes to the bathroom?" Great question. The answer is NO. Since the days of Adam and Eve, it has been the man's job.

WARNING: If you leave the seat up, and she falls into the bowl in the middle of the night, it's you who will (figuratively) be in the shitter.

Toilet Paper Orientation

Are you ready to have your mind blown? Upon marriage, you will find out there is a "right" way to install the toilet paper roll and a "wrong" way. The choices are "over" and "under." Really. It matters to some people.

Your wife will do it the "right" way and you will need to do it her way—even if she does it the wrong way.

(Editor's note: Upstanding people typically prefer the "over" method.)

Toothpaste Squeeze Play

Just as with installing the roll of toilet paper, there is a proper way to squeeze a tube of toothpaste. The odds are that you two won't agree.

One of you will do it the right way—by squeezing up from the very bottom. The other will act like a wild animal and squeeze from the middle of the tube. If your wife is the feral one, politely suggest that she try your amazing squeezing system.

When that fails, just get your own toothpaste. After all, you've got *plenty* of space.

SIDEBAR

"Where Is There Hair?" Quiz

When surveying the Husbands Panel, we discovered that these guys entered marriage entirely unprepared for a common phenomenon: The ubiquity of their wife's hair. It seemed to be everywhere.

It looks great on her head, of course. But it was less appreciated around the house.

Do you know where you might find your wife's hair? Take this handy quiz and find out!

Is your wife's hair _____?

1. In the bathroom sink? — Y or N
2. On the bathroom counter? — Y or N
3. On the bathroom floor? — Y or N
4. In the shower drain? — Y or N
5. On the shower tiles? — Y or N
6. On the bar of soap? — Y or N
7. In her hairbrush? — Y or N
8. In your hairbrush? — Y or N
9. On her bath towel? — Y or N
10. On your bath towel? — Y or N
11. In your bed? — Y or N
12. On the bedroom floor? — Y or N
13. In the kitchen sink? — Y or N
14. On the kitchen counter? — Y or N
15. On the couch? — Y or N
16. In the clothes dryer? — Y or N
17. On your clothes? — Y or N
18. On the dinner table? — Y or N
19. In her car? — Y or N
20. In your car? — Y or N

Answer Key: Questions 1-20: YES!*

(*For No. 4, the judges will also accept, "Holy shit, YES!")

CHAPTER 6

The Bedroom
Let The (Olympic) Games Begin

Now that you and your wife officially share a bedroom ... *va, va, voom* ... let the games begin!

No, silly. Not *those* kinds of games. (We'll be discussing S-E-X in the next chapter.) We're talking about the struggle to secure serenity in your sleeping chamber. And that competition can be fierce.

It's not quite as intense as, say, *The Hunger Games*. But in many ways, it is like the *Olympic Games*. Let's take a look at the events:

Negotiating For Closet And Drawer Space—JUDO
An essential tactic in judo is to use your opponent's strength against them. Try this method to secure bedroom space for your clothes.

Your wife is the all-powerful storage space czar. She knows this. She is proud of this. You will never get a 50-50 split of a shared closet. Or dresser. But if you can stroke her ego the right way, 33% is possible.

Explain how you want to look well-dressed *for her*. And how much better your clothes will look if they get *just a little* more room and aren't all wrinkled.

And when that doesn't work, buy under-the-bed storage bins and cram your stuff there.

Toggling Of The Bedroom Thermostat—TABLE TENNIS

Have you ever watched world-class table tennis (aka ping pong)? The ball goes back and forth and back and forth. It is mesmerizing.

That's what it's like watching your bedroom thermostat. You turn the heat down. Your wife turns it up. Back and forth and back and forth … until you fall asleep and lose the point.

But the match isn't over. When you get up to pee in the middle of the night, you can switch it right back down.

Surmounting Her Pile Of Clothes—HIGH JUMP

Before a night out, dozens of your wife's outfit combinations must be tested. The "losing" clothes can end up on the floor for days in a huge pile that blocks the bed.

What to do? It's time for the high jump. Follow these steps:

1. Run from the doorway towards the bed.

2. Maintain a constant, controlled speed.

The Bedroom

3. As you near the clothes pile, launch into the "Fosbury Flop."

4. Float gracefully over the pile.

5. Pray that you land on the bed.

(Note: Even if successful, you may end up trapped in the bed for days.)

Decluttering An Over-Pillowed Bed—DISCUS THROW

Women LOVE pillows. Your bed has euro pillows, lumbar pillows, boudoir pillows, square cushions and, finally, pillows for sleeping.

What's the point of all these pillows? All you want to do is get in bed!

Time to practice your discus throw. With a shoulder-width stance and a quick spin, launch each pillow from your half of the bed into the nearest corner of the room.

Then *try* to get some sleep. As you'll see, it won't be easy.

Wriggling For Room In The Bed—GYMNASTICS

Gymnasts are nimble, strong and resilient. You will have to be all of the above to stake your territory in the bed.

Be prepared to strike. Slip a leg into open space. Twist your body to nudge hers. Use leverage to gradually *scooch* her just a few inches at a time in the other direction.

If you stick the landing, you could have a *third* of the bed to yourself!

Securing A Fair Share Of The Blanket—WRESTLING

At bedtime, your blanket begins in a neutral position. But once you are asleep, the wrestling match begins.

She starts with a stealth *takedown*—as in *taking* the covers *down* to her side. But you wake up and stop her momentum. An *escape*!

Then you slide towards the middle of the bed, grab the blanket firmly and slowly roll towards your side of the bed. A *reversal*. Victory is yours! … Until the next match 30 minutes later.

Avoiding Contact With Her Cold Feet—FENCING

During the colder months, your wife's feet can become as cold as a steel blade. And as dangerous.

While she is encroaching on your territory in bed, she might—perhaps unknowingly—start the icy foot *attack*. First comes the five-toe *advance* with a *thrust* toward your legs.

En garde, monsieur! Time for your defense. *Parry!* Use an available ankle or shin to block her foot and thwart the first attack.

Next, make a barrier by creating a fold in the blanket at the, er, foot of the bed. Then push her feet as far away as possible. The duel is won!

The Bedroom

Overcoming Her Snoring, Morning Breath And Snooze Button—TRIATHLON

An Olympic triathlete must conquer three distinct disciplines (swimming, biking, running) consecutively without falling victim to the physical and mental toll.

But that's a walk in the park compared to dealing with the early morning bed triathlon: your wife's snoring, morning breath and repetitive snooze button.

Your wife never confessed to being a snorer, because she might not have known. I mean, who is going to tell her? Are you going to tell her?

And while she conscientiously brushes her teeth and flosses, her mouth-breathing into your face at 5 am is not all sunshine and roses.

Finally, because she wants to get every last wink of sleep, she sets her alarm an hour early and hits the snooze button EVERY 15 MINUTES.

Three different challenges. Back to back to back. But don't fret!

Remember those pillows you tossed away? They have a purpose after all! Grab a few and use them to cover your head. *Voila!* Those sounds and smells can't find you now!

CHAPTER 7

Sex
The Keys To Repeat (Funny) Business

It's the chapter that you've been waiting for. It's time to have "the talk." About doing it. Hanky panky. Funny business. Knocking boots. Shenanigans. Doinking. Boinking. Shagging. Making love. S-E-X.

At the beginning of the marriage, the sparks will be flying. You won't be able to keep your hands off each other. You're thankful that your mattress has a good warranty, because the sex is fast and furious. *Bow-chicka-bow-wow.*

You presume it will be like that forever. … But it won't be. Sorry.

"No, no," you say. "We are the exception. It's going to be different with us." … But it won't be. Sorry.

Life simply gets in the way of your once rabbit-like behavior. Work, running a household, kids, familiarity, age. They all factor into the perfectly normal sexual slowdown.

While sexual desire ebbs and flows for both parties over time, it's not unusual for the husband to be the one wanting more lovin' than the wife does.

But that doesn't mean you can't maximize your sexual success rate. The Husband School is here to help. We won't leave you hanging, if you'll pardon the expression.

There are many "tricks of the trade" that guys use to make their wives more receptive to a little action. The Husbands Panel mentioned tactics such as having romantic dinners, drinking champagne, planning tropical vacations, being spontaneous in "risky" locations, providing back massages, giving her a "day off," bringing home flowers, surprising her with spa day gift cards, and more.

Then there is an entire industry of relationship counselors who give husbands more strategic guidance to keep the spark sparking.

Samples include the classics, like "connect emotionally," "share your heart," "laugh together," and even "do your share of the chores." All good advice!

But if you want to get Six Sigma about it, for a husband to maximize sex with his wife, he can learn a lot from how a salesperson maximizes repeat sales.

It all comes down to customer satisfaction.

Let's take a look at the keys to repeat (funny) business:

1. **Determine What Is Important To Your Customer**
   Your wife has specific likes and dislikes, both in and out of the sack. Pay attention. Find out. *Ask her.*

2. **Keep Your Services Top Of Mind**
   Be charming, stay in shape, keep well-groomed, smell great and be affectionate even when there is no love-making on the horizon.

3. **Ask For The Business**
   You don't ask, you don't get. Tell her what's on your mind. Make your pitch. Don't beat around the bush, so to speak.

4. **Provide Outstanding Customer Service**
   Do NOT be selfish. Your wife's needs come first … and then things can focus more on you. This is about repeat business, remember?

5. **Encourage Customer Feedback**
   Over the next day or two, find out: "Was it good for you?" Any suggestions? Requests? Offer her a "make good" at the earliest opportunity. You are willing to bend over backwards (literally) to meet your satisfaction guarantee.

6. **Refresh Your Product Offerings**
   New husbands tend to know only the basics. There's a lot of info

THE NEW HUSBAND'S SURVIVAL GUIDE

out there about a lot of variation. (Note: Pay special attention to "toys." And we're NOT talking about PS5 consoles.) Ignorance is not bliss. Read it. Learn it. Live it.

7. Make It Easy For Your Customer To Reorder

Be charming, stay in shape, keep well-groomed, smell great and be affectionate even when there is no love-making on the horizon. *(Does this sound familiar?)*

8. Ask For The Business Again. And Repeat. Often.

Simple enough, right? With a super-satisfied wife, your goods and services will be in high demand. You could be the top, er, salesman on your block!

Come to think of it, with this sales plan, maybe you two WILL be the "sex-ception" to the slow-down rule. Way to go, Casanova!

You can thank us later.

SIDEBAR

Your Wife's Monthly Visitor

Now that we've covered the subject of S-E-X, we should discuss one of the main obstacles to sexual activity. It's when your wife's "monthly visitor" shows up.

Yep, your mother-in-law can be a major mood-killer. Does she really have to stay over so often?

If that's not frustrating enough, there's another hurdle to overcome: Your wife's menstrual cycle. She is NOT going to be feeling frisky while she is dealing with hormonal fluctuations, cramps, bloating and other fun stuff.

So, during times of premenstrual syndrome (PMS) and the actual period, you may want to put your privates away for a few days and think about how to make your wife more comfortable.

Since no male human has any idea what to do, I asked artificial intelligence to weigh in. Here's what ChatGPT 3.5 had to say about helping your wife get through her monthlies:

Helping Your Wife Cope With PMS And Periods

(From the greatest minds in artificial intelligence)

The Calendar Connoisseur
"Familiarize yourself with the calendar of hormonal events. It's like having a GPS for emotional landscapes. Your navigation skills will be legendary."

(Editor's note: A little creepy, ChatGPT, but go on ...)

The Hormonal Rollercoaster
"Just remember, the ups and downs are a normal part of the ride. Consider it an emotional adventure park, and you're the fearless explorer."

(Editor's note: Buckle up. And prepare to be queasy.)

The Empathy Express
"Understanding and compassion go a long way. Even if you don't fully comprehend the intricacies of hormonal fluctuations, expressing empathy is always a winning strategy."

(Editor's note: Makes sense. Can't really argue with that.)

The Surprise Self-Care Package
"Sometimes, a small gesture like a cozy blanket, a favorite snack, or a heartfelt note can turn a challenging day into a brighter one."

(Editor's note: ChatGPT is on a roll ... Perhaps it's married?)

The Pampering Passport
"Offer relaxation and pampering experiences to help your wife unwind. Massages,

spa days, or simply a quiet evening with her favorite book can be the perfect antidote."

(Editor's note: Suddenly, this period thing is sounding kinda cushy.)

The Snack Attack Defense Strategy
"Stock up on the essentials. When the cravings hit, be the hero with a well-stocked snack arsenal. Chocolate, ice cream, and salty snacks are your allies."

(Editor's note: Will she share with hubby? Asking for a few thousand friends.)

The Pillow Fort Sanctuary
"When PMS turns the world into a chaotic place, offer a cozy retreat where your wife can indulge in comfort and relaxation."

(Editor's note: Hey, ChatGPT … can the dudes have a pillow fort, too?)

The Compliment Carousel
"Shower your wife with compliments on the days when she might not feel her best. Remind her of her awesomeness, period or no period."

(Editor's note: Sure. But sometimes leaving her the hell alone is the best remedy of all. For both of you.)

CHAPTER 8

Social Life
It's Time To Start Seeing Other People

About a month or two after getting married, you will start to get "the itch." At first, there is slight unease. But soon, you will feel stifled and smothered.

Although you love your wife dearly, you realize there is only one solution: It's time to start seeing other people.

No, not romantically, Einstein. *Socially*. Hanging out exclusively with your wife—just the two of you, day after day, night after night—is, well, too much of a good thing.

You are eager to see your old friends again. You are ready to see your family again. You are even willing to see *her* family.

Almost anybody, really.

The challenge is that "your" *(singular possessive)* social life is now "your" *(plural possessive)* social life. And you do not have full control of the calendar. Or the guest list.

THE NEW HUSBAND'S SURVIVAL GUIDE

Let's take a look at who you might be able to socialize with. Just don't expect all of these relationships to stay the same as pre-marriage.

Your Old (Guy) Friends

Does your wife like your guy friends? Well, you will soon learn the difference between her *liking* them and her *tolerating* them. You will still get to see the boys at reunions, important football games, pickup basketball games, etc. But in marriage, "friendship time" will quickly transition into "couples friendship time."

If *her* friends are already part of a couple, the default will have you hanging out with them. Their respective husbands (or boyfriends) are now your new guy friends. Congratulations!

PRO TIP: Find reasons to stay in touch with your old friends. Fantasy football. Gaming. Sharing stupid memes on a WhatsApp chain. When you retire in 40 years, you might have the opportunity to fully reconnect with these guys.

Your Old (Gal) Friends

We turned to the internet to see if it's okay for married men to keep in touch with their old, platonic, female friends. WikiHow.com was quite emphatic:

"Is it okay for a married man to have female friends?

"Yes; in fact, it's healthy! You should always encourage your husband to have friends, no matter what gender they are. As long as your husband and his friends respect your relationship, there shouldn't be any problems."

HAHAHAHAHAHAHA!!!! (deep breath)

HAHAHAHAHAHAHA!!!!

Uh, NO, WikiHow. That's not how it works. Your pre-marriage female friends will rarely, if ever, be a thing moving forward.

Your Parents

Even if you haven't lived with your parents for a decade, your marriage serves as a kind of separation from them. And separation anxiety happens to parents, too.

Now that you're married, you will be asked to equitably allocate your parent time. This includes dividing holidays, like Mother's Day, Thanksgiving and Christmas. Good luck with that.

Happily, there will usually be a few obligatory family gatherings—Billy's graduation, Aunt Mary's big birthday bash, etc.—so you'll get to see siblings, cousins, aunts, uncles, grandparents, etc.

THE NEW HUSBAND'S SURVIVAL GUIDE

Your mother will struggle with the relationship transition more than your father will. Dad will act pretty much the same. But Mom, who has been *mothering* you forever, will find it very difficult to stop.

And your wife is NOT going to like it. The missus is the new sheriff in town, and she doesn't want a deputy.

It's best that you (kindly) tell Mom that ASAP. But you won't. Because you're a wuss and you're afraid to hurt her feelings. And you know it won't work. Either way, from now on, the *Mother vs. Wife* tension will be YOUR fault. Ugh.

Your Siblings
It's cool. Nothing really changes.

Her Parents
After you negotiate holidays and other visits, you get to spend time with your in-laws. That's generally okay, as long as they don't consider you a low-life who isn't good enough for their daughter. (In that case, you have a few years to prove them wrong.)

Your father-in-law will be chill, happy to talk sports and regale you with rambling stories from his college days. But he's harmless.

Your mother-in-law, naturally, will be the tricky one. Not because of her interactions with you. It's due to her relationship with your wife.

The two of them absolutely, 100% love each other. And much of the time, they don't particularly *like* each other. Especially when your mother-in-law acts like the mother hen of your new household. This will drive your wife crazy.

Good news: This will NOT be your fault. Bad news: It will be your problem.

Steer clear while the two of them are bickering. And be prepared to listen to your wife vent about it later. And then again, repeatedly, over the next few days.

(Remember what we learned in Chapter 2: Just nod often and keep your mouth shut.)

Her Siblings
It's cool. Nothing really changes.

Conclusion
All things considered, maybe it's not so bad just hanging out with your wife. She's a lot of fun. And it's SO much easier.

So make that dinner reservation for two. Get a pair of tickets for the comedy show. Keep those Date Nights coming!

You can see those "other people" some other time.

CHAPTER 9

Communication
Can You Speak Venusian?

The classic pop-psych book *Men Are from Mars, Women Are from Venus* uses the metaphor in its title to explain that men and women are basically from different planets. As a result, the way they communicate is vastly different.

(That's obvious, linguistically. Venusian and Martian are very dissimilar languages. So things will get lost in translation. … And don't start joking about that phony Klingon nonsense. This is a serious book.)

That's why The Husband School has researched some of the key areas where men and women have communication differences, so you'll be prepared when they pop up.

Expressing Desires
When indicating what they want, husbands are often direct. Subtlety is not at the fore.

With wives, however, it's all about unspoken expectations. Hubby must be part detective and part mind reader.

You will be perpetually on the lookout for emotional cues and stealthy signals. The process is as scientific as reading tea leaves or tarot cards. And equally as accurate.

Her quick glance will mean something. Her subtle sigh will say something else. But what is it? That's for you, the Psychic Spouse, to figure out.

That entails trial and error. With an emphasis on the latter.

(Editor's note: Wives are experts at not saying what they truly mean. It's as if husbands need a Wife Translator. Good news! The Wife Translator is just a few pages away!)

Sharing Feelings

When dealing with stress or conflict, husbands can become aloof and introspective. The question, "How are you feeling?" gets either a one-word answer or a tepid grunt.

When some wives (not all!) get the same question in the same circumstances, it can be like watching a reality TV show. The emotion flows. There are dramatic reenactments, with detailed commentary about what the characters did and who is to blame. (You may be implicated.) There are heroes and villains. And tears. Plenty of tears.

Hang in there. You will NOT be able to fast-forward this episode.

Communication

Seeking Quiet Time

After a long, hard day of work, you might want to simply chill out in front of the TV. Or get to sleep early. You desperately need some quiet time to reset your brain.

Your wife will have a different plan. This will be when she chooses to engage you in deep conversation. About deep subjects:
- The meaning of life
- Securing world peace
- Solving world hunger
- Extended family dynamics
- Achieving life goals
- Dreams for the future
- And (*gasp*) the state of your relationship

These will not be short conversations. Because wives are NOT concise storytellers …

Storytelling

With regard to storytelling, husbands sprint to the point: Here's. What. Happened.

For wives, however, a story can be like a marathon. You might endure a maze of information before you can even see the

THE NEW HUSBAND'S SURVIVAL GUIDE

finish line. There are twists and turns and tangents galore. It may all be worth it in the end, but each story is an exercise in patience.

Sometimes you might not have that patience. So, you'll need the ability to look like you're listening—even when you're not. Depending on whether it's a good-news story or a bad-news story, use one or more of these:

- **The Nod and Smile System**—It signals that you're actively listening, as long as you don't grin widely during a negative plot twist.

- **The Phony Focus Face**—Look slightly puzzled and perhaps a bit concerned. Squinted eyes and a furrowed brow prove you are fully invested.

- **The Generic Response Generator**—Sprinkle in an occasional "Wow!" or "You're kidding!" during her story to indicate you are totally following along.

- **The Dramatic Eyebrow Raise**—If her voice goes up an octave, quickly raise one (or both) of your eyebrows. It demonstrates you are as shocked as she is.

- **The Repeat and Retreat Plan**—Every now and then, repeat the last few words that she said, so you get a "Yes, exactly!" response … before she keeps going.

- **The Contemplative Head Tilt**—If you haven't reacted for a while, break out the head tilt. For added effect, stare into space. You are now deeply pondering the implications of this important story. What a great husband you are!

Constructive Criticism

Husbands don't love getting criticized. But after being told that our favorite shirt is ratty or that we could benefit from a little deodorant, we accept the criticism and move on.

That is NOT how it works with wives. One hundred compliments can be wiped away instantly by one criticism. Even a half-hearted compliment will be considered a criticism. And it will not be forgotten quickly. More accurately, it will never be forgotten.

So tread VERY lightly if you have some constructive criticism about her cooking, driving, clothing, makeup, cleanliness, technology proficiency, exercise habits or her relatives. Any of these can lead to the one thing we aim to avoid at all costs—an argument.

What's the big deal about arguments? Well, that topic is a chapter in itself. Don't worry. We'll help you navigate those, too.

Even if the husband and wife are speaking two completely different extraterrestrial languages.

SIDEBAR

Wife Translator

Why is husband-wife communication so challenging? As discussed in Chapter 9, a husband often has to do detective work simply to decipher his wife's unspoken expectations.

But her spoken expectations can be even more baffling.

That's because you never quite know if she is saying what she means—or the opposite of what she means. Or somewhere in between.

Thankfully, The Husband School's patent-pending Wife Translator is here to help! If you learn the following key phrases (and their translated meanings), you will be able to speak "Wife" on at least an eighth-grade level.

Wife Translator Phrases

Wife: "I'm fine."
Translator: "I'm NOT fine. I'm the opposite of fine—primarily because you haven't figured out why I'm not fine."

Wife: "Be honest. I promise I won't get angry."
Translator: "Choose your words carefully, bub. If you speak your mind, I am going to be very angry."

Wife: "We need to talk."
Translator: "I need to talk. You need to listen."

Wife: "Do I look okay?"
Translator: "Do I look 10/10 hot? Because that's what I want to hear."

Wife: "Nothing is wrong."
Translator: "Plenty is wrong. And I can't believe you don't know why it's your fault."

Wife: "Do whatever you want."
Translator: "Do the opposite of what you want, which is what I want."

Wife: "You don't need to buy me anything."
Translator: "But if you don't, I will probably never forgive you."

Wife: "I'm tired."
Translator: "No sexy time for you tonight. Try again tomorrow."

Wife: "I have a headache."
Translator: See "I'm tired" above

Wife: "She's cute, huh?"
Translator: "I can see you looking at her, and you better stop now."

Wife: "We need to fix that."
Translator: "YOU need to fix that."

Wife: "It's your decision."
Translator: "It's our decision, and you better take my side."

Wife: "Maybe …"
Translator: "No."

SIDEBAR

Wife: "Are you hungry?"
Translator: "I'm hungry!"

Wife: "Are you going to eat that?"
Translator: "When are you going to share that with me?"

Wife: "I don't want any of your dessert."
Translator: "I'll save you half. Or slightly less."

Wife: "Are you going dressed like that?"
Translator: "Change your clothes. You look ridiculous!"

Wife: "Don't worry about it."
Translator: "You need to fix this!"

Wife: Multiple one-word answers
Translator: Storm clouds on the horizon

Wife: "I told you so …"
Translator: "I don't like to gloat … Well, actually, I do like to gloat. But next time, listen to me."

Wife: "It's okay."
Translator: "It is so NOT okay. It is as far from okay as possible."

Wife: "I'll be ready in five minutes."
Translator: "Check back in 30."

Wife: "I'll do it later."
Translator: "Don't hold your breath."

Wife: "You don't have to ask, just go ahead and do it."
Translator: "You have my permission … just as long as you ask."

Wife: "I am not pouting."
Translator: "I will keep pouting until you apologize."

Wife: "I need a new pair of shoes."
Translator: "I'm going to buy six new pairs of shoes plus a pair of boots."

Wife: "We could do that."
Translator: "That ain't happening."

Wife: "What do you want for dinner?"
Translator: "I've got nothing. Let's order in."

Wife: "Which one do you like?"
Translator: "I've chosen the one I like. If you're lucky, we will agree. If not, I'm buying the one I like."

Wife: "I don't need any help with the housework."
Translator: "I am NOT a servant. Pick up the damn vacuum."

Wife: "Do you want to get into bed early tonight?"
Translator: Your luck might have *finally* changed … for the better.

CHAPTER 10

Arguments
"My Wife Is Never Wrong"

According to mental health professionals, arguments between husbands and wives are perfectly normal. In fact, they are (allegedly) *helpful*. Yippee!

Says one clinical psychologist, "Conflict is an opportunity for two people to actually grow and understand themselves better."* Hooray!

But doesn't that kinda sound like "Whatever doesn't kill you makes you stronger"? Do you really want to test your luck like that?

A legit, hash-it-out, husband-wife argument ruins your day (or days). You will both be grouchy, wandering aimlessly with a pit in your stomach while being totally weird around each other.

Your wife might punish you with the "silent treatment," which sounds refreshing, but really isn't. She might also hit you with the occasional "icy stare of death." It will put a shiver through your entire being.

---

*Maria Thestrup, PhD on EverydayHealth.com

THE NEW HUSBAND'S SURVIVAL GUIDE

Inevitably, mercifully, the argument will finally come to an end. Once someone apologizes. ... And that someone will be you.

When it comes to arguments, remember The Husband School's motto: UXOR MEA NON ERRAT. That's Latin for "My Wife Is Never Wrong." (Or close enough.) The ancient Romans knew it then. We know it now.

If you accept that your wife is never wrong, it will minimize the number of arguments you have. Because, well, what's the point?

True, this won't fully eliminate arguments, because there will be differences of opinion. And people *do* need to express themselves. According to marriage.com,* here are the top 10 things couples argue about:

1. Sex
2. Money
3. Family
4. Parenting Styles
5. Talking to Ex-Partners
6. Sharing Private Information with Third Parties
7. Religion
8. Being Possessive

9. Choice of Friends

10. Do We Have to Discuss Aunt Bertha's Goiter While I'm Trying to Watch The Game?**

Thankfully, there are ways to avoid dragged-out arguments. Here are a few tips:

Don't Share Everything On Your Mind
You don't have to mention how the guys in the office are drooling over the smokin'-hot new associate. There is a thing called "too much information." Shhh.

Timing Is Everything
Pick your spots. When your wife is weary or frustrated after a tough day, that is NOT the time to suggest you want to go camping with the guys next weekend. Read the room!

Fight Fair
Attack problems without attacking each other. "Win the battle, lose the war, sleep on the couch" is not a great result.

"Never Go To Bed Angry"
This old saw is accurate. If your wife is steaming mad at 10 pm,

---

*https://www.marriage.com/advice/relationship/couple-arguing/

**Okay. We made that one up. But it applies.

THE NEW HUSBAND'S SURVIVAL GUIDE

imagine how she'll be eight hours later after spending the whole night tossing, turning and simmering over how pigheaded you are.

The Power Of "Yes, Dear"

If you find yourself on the verge of an argument, say "Yes, dear" as quickly—*and sincerely*—as possible. (Try not to be too robotic.) With luck, the crisis will be averted!

- ▶ "Will you please be more quiet when I'm trying to sleep?"— > "Yes, dear."
- ▶ "Can you please put the dirty dishes in the dishwasher and not in the sink?"— > "Yes, dear."
- ▶ "Can my mother stay over next week?"— > "Um, let me get back to you on that."

Avoid "Confrontational" Facial Expressions

Even if you say nothing, you might be saying too much.

You should be fine, as long as you do NOT do any of the following:

Arguments

Roll your eyes, raise your eyebrows, furrow your brow, smirk, stare into space, clench your jaw, smile too tightly, glare, sigh, frown, blink rapidly, look away, scowl, sneer, squint, raise your chin, look at the clock or glance at your phone. Simple!

If you *do* have an argument, and you are ready to bring it to an end, it's time to deliver your apology. Make sure it's a good one.

According to experts,* for a proper apology, follow this process:

Step 1: Acknowledge your partner's hurt or anger

Step 2: Apologize for what you said or did

Step 3: Briefly explain your own motives and perspective

Step 4: Apologize again

Example: "I recognize that you are upset, and I am sorry that I got home at 2 am last night. I thought I would stop at the bar for one quick drink with the boys, but I was wrong. You see, Billy wanted to play pool, and then Tim got into a fistfight with the bouncer, and we all had to go bail him out of jail. By that time we were starving, so we stopped at the diner for eggs. And I lost track of the time. But, anyway, I am so sorry.

---

*Healthy Relationships Utah; https://extension.usu.edu/hru/blog/how-to-apologize-to-your-partner

THE NEW HUSBAND'S SURVIVAL GUIDE

You are amazing and beautiful and I love you SO much. And I'll never do it again. I promise!"

That's a quality apology! This template will work for almost anything.

Just make sure to have it handy for next week's argument. You're going to need it.

SIDEBAR

Wife Hacks

We've gone almost the entire book without writing the phrase, "Happy wife, happy life." Because it's such an overused, tired, stale cliché. But it's also true.

If the missus is in good spirits, and is generally pleased with her husband, your life will be SO much better. Therefore, it behooves you to do the work to keep her happy. (Or at least keep her happy with you.)

How do you do that? Broadly speaking, don't be a dick. Treat your wife better than anyone else you care about. Even when she annoys the crap out of you.

More specifically, make a concerted effort to show her that you care. Random acts of kindness will do the trick.

You need examples? Okay, rookie. Here is a list of "Wife Hacks"—which we define as small gestures that will keep your wife feeling warm and fuzzy for days. And could keep you out of the penalty box for just as long.

Premium Wife Hacks

"Just Because" Flowers
It's not her birthday. It's not your anniversary. But you bring home a bouquet for her anyway. Brownie points obtained! … When she asks you why you got her flowers, you reply, "Just because I was thinking of you." Now the brownie points are off the chart. You are a freaking hero! It's the best $25 you'll ever spend.

Back Massages With No Sexpectations
While you're watching TV together, ask her if she wants a back (or foot) massage. When she skeptically asks what you expect in return, make it clear that you are NOT looking for some lovin'. You just want to make her happy. She may swoon. … And after the massage, if she wants some action, who are you to say no?

Surprise Love Notes
Are you leaving for work before she gets up? That's the perfect time to leave a sticky note on the bathroom mirror, on the fridge or in her car. It almost doesn't matter what you write. (But gushy is good.) It shows you are thinking about her. What a guy!

Random Acts Of Affection
You're on the couch, watching TV. You hear her in the kitchen, fixing herself a snack. You get up. Walk to the kitchen. Grab her in a warm embrace. Give her a big smooch on the lips. Tell her you love her. And

then go back to the couch with no explanation. ... Damn, you are smooth. And quite a keeper!

Hidden Gifts
You don't need jewelry to make a splash. Secretly buy a new lipstick. Or even a pack of M&Ms. Wrap the gift with a small bow. Slip it into her purse. Wait patiently for her to discover it. Bask in the glory of being her Prince Charming.

Honorable Mention Wife Hacks:

- Make surprise dinner reservations at her favorite restaurant
- Compliment her in public whenever you introduce her
- Do one of "her" chores while she is out of the house
- Remember (and celebrate) "pseudo anniversaries" (first date, engagement, etc.)
- Tell her regularly that she looks great—especially after a haircut
- Complete that pesky DIY project she really wants done
- Text her occasional emoji-only love notes
- Thank her for being an amazing wife
- Hold her hand when you're out shopping
- Write a silly poem or song about her
- Say "I Love You" often—and tell her why

See, this husband stuff isn't too complicated after all!

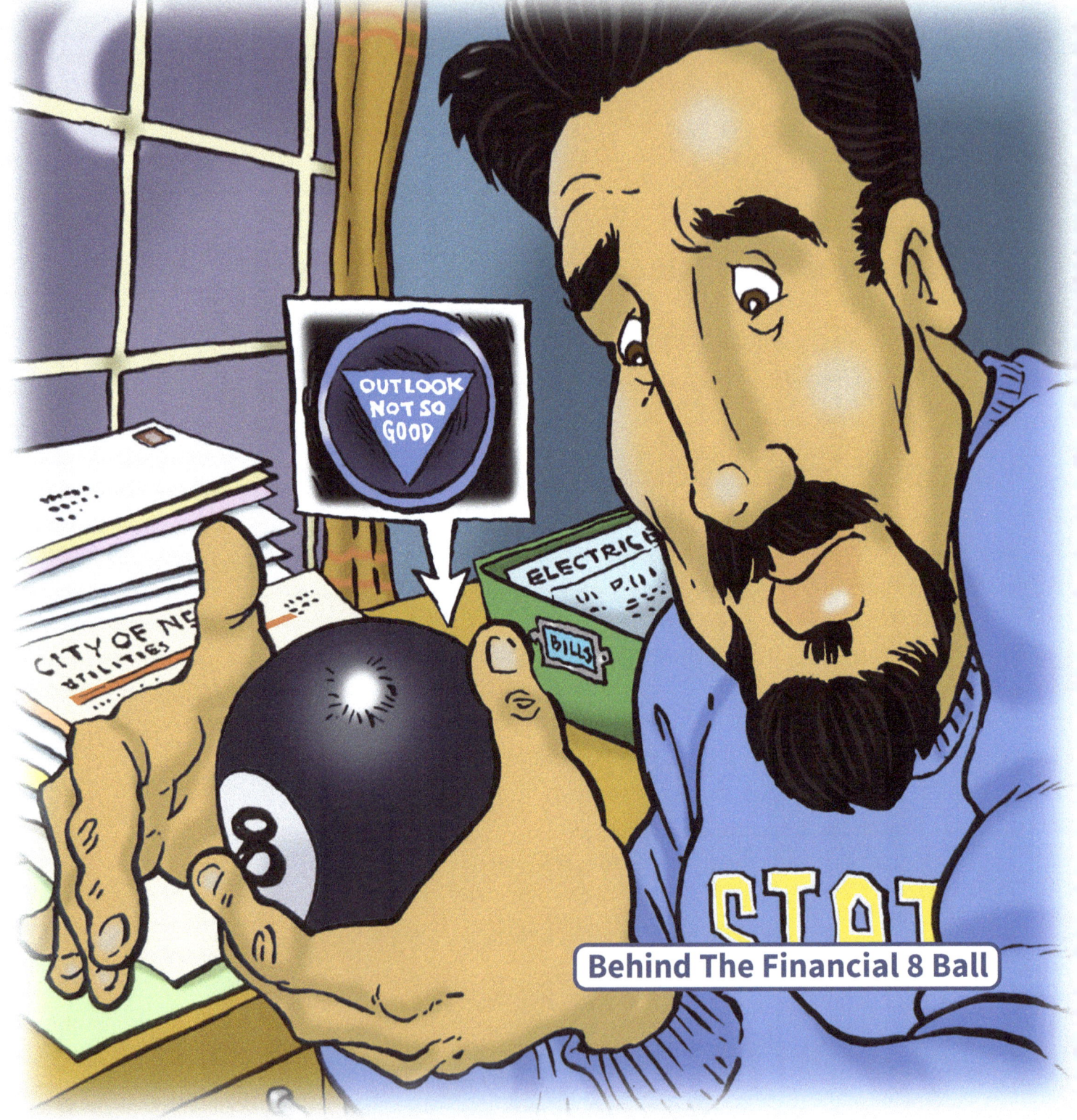

CHAPTER 11

Money Matters
Ask The Magic 8 Ball

In the previous chapter, we learned that money is the second most frequent topic for husbands and wives to argue about. But will you and your wife quarrel over household finances?

Truthfully, we don't know. So we asked someone, er, *something* that does. The Magic 8 Ball.™

(You remember Magic 8 Ball, right? That black orb with spooky blue liquid inside and a 20-sided die floating around to answer your questions? Its track record is unparalleled.)

Few people know that Magic 8 Ball is a certified financial advisor. Let's learn from its wisdom:

Will You And Your Wife Argue Over Money?
Magic 8 Ball: *"IT IS DECIDEDLY SO"*

Sorry. But the odds were against you. Think about all that's involved: budgeting, saving, spending, debt, investments, careers, work/life

THE NEW HUSBAND'S SURVIVAL GUIDE

balance, (potentially) raising kids, retirement and other long-term goals. You guys aren't going to agree on everything.

Not to worry! You'll be fine, as long as your spending vs. savings levels happen to align.

Will Your Spending vs. Savings Levels Align?
Magic 8 Ball: *"OUTLOOK NOT SO GOOD"*

Since you two decided to get married, you likely have similar values and interests. But that doesn't mean you'll have similar attitudes toward spending. "Spenders" tend to live in the moment, while "Savers" have an eye on the future.

What does that mean for potential bickering? Here's the Spenders vs. Savers grid:

Two Savers — Life is a bit boring, but safe and secure. Low stress. Few arguments. ✅

Two Spenders — Tons of fun, living on the edge. Low stress— until the bills come due and sparks fly. ⚠️

Wife Saver/ Husband Spender — You have lots of cool stuff, and an angry wife. Stressful. ⚠️

Husband Saver/ Wife Spender — She is happy. You are not. You are screwed. ❌

Money Matters

If You're A Saver And Your Wife's A Spender, Can You Get Her To Change?

Magic 8 Ball: *"MY SOURCES SAY NO."*

You can try discussing long-term goals and the need to save for a rainy day.

Example: *"Sweetheart, if you spend a little less on shoes, when we retire, we might not have to live in a VAN down by the RIVER!"*

But spenders are gonna spend.

Happily, there is some consolation:
- Your wife's "retail therapy" might be cheaper than her going to a shrink
- She will be racking up tons of miles on her credit cards
- Amazon will be thankful for her business
- She will always have fashionable clothes to wear
- Almost single-handedly, she is boosting the U.S. economy

Plus you'll get to make friends with both the UPS and FedEx drivers.

And who doesn't need more friends?

Is "Girl Math" Real?

Magic 8 Ball: *"YOU MAY RELY ON IT"*

THE NEW HUSBAND'S SURVIVAL GUIDE

What is "Girl Math"? With regard to shopping, it's the belief that spending more means saving more. YOU might know that buying two dresses at 25% off is NOT cheaper than buying one dress.

But can your wife really pass up such a steal of a deal?

Other examples of Girl Math:
- Anything paid for with cash is free (because it doesn't affect the credit card bill)
- Anything under $5 is free (even if you buy 20 of those items)
- If an item is on sale, you're making a profit (and that's like earning money)
- Always buy more to get the free shipping (which saves a lot of money)
- You must take part in a "buy one, get one half-off" sale (or you are losing money)

Of course, it's possible that your wife is NOT the spender in the family, and it's YOU who likes to splurge. That leads to the next question ...

Do You Really Need That $2,800

Money Matters

Milwaukee Brand M18 FUEL 18V Lithium-Ion Brushless Cordless 1-1/2 Inch Lineman Magnetic Drill High Demand Kit With Two 8.0Ah Batteries?
Magic 8 Ball: *"SIGNS POINT TO YES"*

Well, duh. Of course you do. It "drills faster than the number one corded competitor, delivers the strongest magnetic hold on 1/4 inch steel providing a safer drilling environment in this material, and drills over seventy-five 13/16 inch holes per charge." Badass!

Your wife will certainly understand.

Should You Two Have Separate Bank Accounts?
Magic 8 Ball: *"CONCENTRATE AND ASK AGAIN"*

Um, okay.

Should You Two Have Separate Bank Accounts?
Magic 8 Ball: *"BETTER NOT TELL YOU NOW"*

Never mind. We at The Husband School recommend it. Separate accounts for "fun money" and a joint account for big stuff. Remember though, it's all really one pool of money that you have to share.

Rule of thumb: If a purchase costs more than $500, discuss it with your spouse first. … Unless, of course, it's the Milwaukee brand

M18 FUEL 18V Lithium-Ion Brushless Cordless 1-1/2 inch Lineman Magnetic Drill High Demand Kit with Two 8.0Ah Batteries.

Should You Be Upset If Your Wife Makes More Money Than You Do?

Magic 8 Ball: *"MY REPLY IS NO"*

Correct, again, Magic 8 Ball! Does your wife make more money than you? Congrats! You've got it made. Let her keep raking in the Benjamins and stay out of her way!

Is Raising Kids Really, Really Expensive?

Magic 8 Ball: *"YES"*

If Magic 8 Ball had a "HELL, YES" answer, that would be more accurate. But, raising kids is more than just really, really expensive. It's also extremely costly, as in costing you your sleep, peace, youthful glow and sanity. And your social life. And your sex life.

Of course, parenthood is not 100% a bad thing. Probably not even 90% a bad thing. Which we'll dig into deeper in the next chapter …

CHAPTER 12

Making Babies
The Parent Trap

Just like you aren't *obligated* to have children, we aren't obligated to write about having kids.

After all, this is *The New Husband's Survival Guide*. It is NOT *The New Father's Survival Guide*. That's a whole different book. Or books. (Which we might write soon.)

But since we are here to help, we will indulge you with some guidance. Especially concerning the baby-raising part, if you are so inclined.

Because if starting a marriage is like playing checkers, starting a family is like playing three-dimensional chess. With little to no sleep, and a lot of spit-up on your clothes.

Let's start at the beginning: Where do babies come from?

Well, when Mommy and Daddy love each other very much, they hug and kiss in a very special way … and nine months later a baby comes out of Mommy's tummy.

Making Babies

Oh, you knew that. Okay. Here's a tougher question: When does the baby-making process begin?

Well, when Mommy says so.

Starting on the day of the marriage proposal, your wife has been weighing her biological clock, your collective financial situation and multiple horoscopes to determine the right time to start making babies.

You will be told, with very little notice, when that time arrives.

(One example—Wife: "I'm out of birth control pills." Husband: "Can't you just go to the pharmacy?" Wife: "I don't plan on getting any more." Husband: "Why?" … pause … realization … "Oh!")

Based on her ovulation schedule, you will be instructed when and where you are required to be for intercourse.

At first, you will think that having your wife demand sex on a regular, scheduled basis is the best thing ever. Until you realize you are merely the sperm donor in this enterprise.

In other words, this is not about romance. There will be no pre-game sweet talk or cuddling. This is about getting the job done. You are the hired help. Get busy, lad!

THE NEW HUSBAND'S SURVIVAL GUIDE

Once your wife gets pregnant, she will go into Mothering Mode. Nurturing. Emotional. Protective. You're still her favorite person, but now it's a tie with a fetus.

For weeks, especially in the first trimester, she will feel nauseated. It's not your fault, but it is your problem. You will get her whatever she needs to eat and drink, and do whatever she needs to feel better.

You will provide back massages and foot rubs and blanket forts. You will do it and not complain. Otherwise, everyone will think you're an asshole.

As the pregnancy goes on, she will become big. Very big. She will complain to you that she looks like an overgrown hippo. You will say, "You look radiant!" Do not stray from that. It's the one phrase that seems to work.

As the months crawl along, she will become uncomfortable, cranky and irritable. When she yells at you for five minutes straight for leaving the peanut butter jar on the counter, you will reply, "Yes, dear. I'm sorry." And then you will go hide.

Good news: Her breasts will become larger, rounder and even more glorious.

Bad news: They will almost certainly be off-limits to you.

Making Babies

Throughout her pregnancy, your kid-less friends will feel bad for you. Your buddies with kids will revel in their *schadenfreude*. "Ha, ha. It's your turn!"

Eventually, the baby arrives! And then the situation gets worse.

You are now playing second fiddle to a toothless stranger who started squatting in your home. This intruder has an attitude problem and is constantly crying or crapping or demanding to be fed. Now!

(But you will put up with the little troublemaker because, magically, you will have fallen in love with her. Or him.)

You will not sleep until the baby learns to sleep.

You will fake being asleep in the middle of the night hoping that your wife will take care of the baby. She will not be fooled.

Through bleary eyes, you and your

THE NEW HUSBAND'S SURVIVAL GUIDE

sleep-deprived wife will bicker about a wide range of issues, including:

- Baby sleep strategies
- Various parenting techniques
- 2 am diaper changes
- Who is doing more work to take care of the baby
- How much it costs for all the baby gear
- Why the new grandparents are constantly coming over
- The need for some personal time to unwind
- If and when you'll ever have Date Night again
- If and when you'll ever have sex again

You will fondly remember nine months earlier when your wife demanded sex from you early and often. Damn, those were good times.

Silver lining: You will learn important life skills. Such as changing diapers, applying diaper rash ointment, folding a stroller, feeding and burping a baby, cleaning up puke, adjusting a crib and begging a baby to stop crying.

PRO TIP: Never offer to "babysit" your own kid. If you do, every mother within a five-mile radius will come over to scold you. Or worse.

Once you muddle your way through newborn chaos and infancy

mayhem, it gets slightly easier. Until the kid is mobile. And then you are on 24/7 prison guard duty.

What comes next? Well, in a blink of an eye, you'll have:

- Toddler Escapades—featuring temper tantrums and the "terrible twos"
- Preschool Adventures—with lessons on acute parental separation anxiety
- Elementary School Exploration—when your wife turns into a ferocious mama bear
- Teenage Turmoil—starring frequent, household-wide mood swings
- College Capers—which you've been saving up for, right?
- Adulthood Launch—as you pray to the heavens that your kid will take flight

Before you know it, you and your wife will have reached the Empty Nest Transition.

Which means, at long last, that you can have sex again.

CONCLUSION

Looking Back

What a whirlwind it has been! A few days ago, in the company of dozens of family members and friends, you and your bride celebrated your 50th wedding anniversary. Congratulations!

What a bash it was. Food, fun and a flood of memories. A great night for a wonderful couple.

But now, you two are having a typically quiet evening at home, sitting on the couch together, watching her favorite game show, "The Wheel of Fortune," with host Pat Sajak III. The missus still usually figures out the puzzles well before any of the contestants do.

You glance her way, and she smiles back. Even after all these years, she still has the same sparkle in her eyes. It's what you first noticed the day you met. Man, that was a long time ago.

And what a long, strange trip it has been.

You thought you were worldly on your wedding day, but you didn't realize how naive you truly were. You had NO IDEA what you were getting into. You didn't know so many aspects of marriage, such as:

THE NEW HUSBAND'S SURVIVAL GUIDE

- The honeymoon period (and how it doesn't last)
- Rookie mistakes that husbands make
- That girls are gross, too
- How your wife would change over time
- Tussles over household chores
- The amount of (her) hair that would be everywhere
- Battles for space in the bedroom and bathroom
- The keys to keeping your sex life rocking
- Trying to decipher what your wife really means
- Learning how to argue and apologize
- Clever "wife hacks" that would leave her feeling happy for days
- Figuring out household finances
- Making babies and what happens next

If there had only been some sort of resource back then. A "survival guide" for new husbands would have been extremely useful.

Even priceless.

But you two eventually figured out things, both big and small.

Some examples? Let's start with the small ones:

Who knew that using separate blankets would be a nighttime game-changer? And then, when you moved into the bigger house, you invested in a king-sized bed. The best!

Looking Back

The splurge for a good house cleaning service removed a ton of tension from the day-to-day. Hiring that financial planner was worth 10x the price. And when you transitioned to separate bathrooms, marital harmony reached an all-time high.

Eureka!

But right now, as you gaze at your wife relaxing happily on the couch, you're pondering the BIG lessons you hadn't considered when you proposed. Such as:

- Whenever you were feeling down, she would always be the one to pick you up
- How she helped you make good decisions when you were building your career
- How she pushed you away from making bad decisions, like when you wouldn't go to the doctor (but really needed to)
- The way you two became a fiercely united team to ensure that your kids were loved, supported and prepped for a purposeful life
- The fact that—even after 50+ years—you would still greatly enjoy each other's company and conversation

There was no guarantee everything would turn out this way. Some of it was luck. A lot of it was love. The rest was because you married well.

Before you got hitched, your then-girlfriend insisted that you were perfect. That she loved you exactly as you were.

And once you got married, she immediately started trying to change you.

And she was right.

She was right about almost everything.

About how you needed a little self-improvement. When it was time to get married. When to buy a house. When to get a dog. When to have kids. How to raise them. How to balance work and home. How to build a life together. How to love.

You literally couldn't have done it without her. And you're glad you didn't try.

But would you do it all over again if you could?

In a heartbeat. As it turned out, you wouldn't change a thing.

MEET THE BOOK TEAM

About The Author

Rick Resnick is the founder and headmaster of The Husband School.™ As a longtime writer, marketer and rapscallion, he understands the importance of choosing the right words and strategies for successful husbanding (and parenting). He lives in Pennsylvania with his brilliant, charming, stunning and unerring trophy wife, Carolyn, and their lovable dog, Rocket. You can connect with Rick at **husbandschool.co** or via The Husband School's social media channels.

About The Illustrator

An award-winning cartoonist, illustrator and writer, **Dan Foote** has entertained countless thousands with his work, including his stint as editorial cartoonist at the *Dallas Times Herald*. His latest project is called "Doodlin' With Dan," designed to teach kids how to have fun drawing. The veteran husband and father lives with his wife, Amy, in Colorado, close to their kids and six grandkids. Dan can be reached at **doodlinwithdan.com**.

About The Designer

A pioneer in digital publishing, **Tom Carling** launched Carling Design with a focus on magazine design and quickly won acclaim producing native advertising inserts for *Sports Illustrated* and other titles. More recently, working directly for publishers or in partnership with book packagers, Tom has produced hundreds of children's trade and school/library nonfiction books. Tom works out of his loft in lower Manhattan, close to his daughter, Tian. You can contact Tom at **carlingdesign.com**.

But wait...
there's MORE great husband stuff from The Husband School!

Visit us at **HusbandSchool.co** for:

- Husband News & Notes
- Comedian Clips
- Gear & Gifts
- Cool Merch
- Relationship Resource Center
- Information on our next book(s)
- And stuff we haven't even dreamed up yet

That's **HusbandSchool.co**.
(Remember, leave off the last "m." That's the "m" for "matrimony.")

www.ingramcontent.com/pod-product-compliance
Lightning Source LLC
Chambersburg PA
CBHW042358030426

42337CB00032B/5145